Making Soft Toys

Making Soft Toys

Gillian Lockwood

Studio Vista   London

Watson-Guptill Publications   New York

General Editors Janey O'Riordan and Brenda Herbert
© Gillian Lockwood 1967
Published in London by Studio Vista Limited
Blue Star House, Highgate Hill, London N 19
and in New York by Watson-Guptill Publications
165 West 46th Street, New York 10036
Distributed in Canada by General Publishing Co. Ltd
30 Lesmill Road, Don Mills, Toronto, Canada
Reprinted 1969
Library of Congress Catalog Card Number 67–13737
Set in Folio Grotesque 8 and 9 pt.
Printed and bound in Great Britain by
Bookprint Limited, Crawley, Sussex

SBN: 289. 27927. 5

Contents

The photographs were taken by Geoffrey Drury

Introduction

Stuffed rag toys have been part of children's play material for a very long time. They were made at home from materials left over from making clothes or household furnishings. There would be no pattern for the toy; the maker worked out the design, which was often limited by the materials available. Early rag toys were usually very simple, but this did not matter to the imaginative child.

The condition of most of the examples which still survive show them to have been very real playthings which were much loved, and not just possessions to be looked at.

The aim of this book is to interest the reader in making soft toys which are more exciting and original than can be bought. The toys illustrated in the book are only starting points to toymaking, and some of the marginal drawings show how the patterns can be developed to suit individual needs.

The older child likes the idea of a toy specially made for him, and can contribute by suggesting colours and kinds of materials. This can be developed as the child's own ability at needlework improves, and with help and guidance some of the simple toys will be within his or her capabilities. I suggest that the flat animals, cat, fish, and the simple bear, are the best toys for a beginner of limited needlework experience.

What are soft toys made of?

Before choosing which toy to make, think about the materials which toys can be made from.

It helps enormously if you keep a 'bit' bag. Looking through a varied collection of materials can give you an idea of the 'feel' of different materials and how they contrast in texture as well as pattern and colour. Velvets, corduroy, tweed, smooth cotton, satin, all can be exciting. Try experimenting by putting pieces of different colour and texture together.

Try associating them with a toy; one piece may be perfect for one part of a particular toy and the rest will just build up from there. The toad given in this book was made from a remnant of a blouse, and the dots so strongly suggested a toad that a toad had to take shape; the material for his underside was bought to blend in. The hedgehog was suggested by just sufficient long-haired brown wool being left over from making the bear to make his back; his face and underparts were made from felt. The mouse was made from a small scrap of gold velvet left over from a cushion. Here, the feel of velvet was suggestive of mouse, as well as the colour.

After a while you will come to look at interesting materials as 'trousers', 'coats', etc. Pieces of material which already have 'associations' for the child can also help to give that extra something; a doll's dress can be made from a remnant of the child's own dress. Toys made in this way are more exciting than if you set out to buy specially for a toy, which is why I have not given required lengths for materials.

Don't be put off if you have not got a rag bag - buy for one toy and you will have started one, and if you mention you are making toys to your friends, you will have numerous pieces given to you.

If you have to buy the material for your toy, cut out the pattern for it, lay it on newspaper folded to 36" or 54" wide, as applicable, and measure the length you will need.

If the toy you want to make is for a very small child, it should be washable. Colours should be fixed and materials washable, shrink-proof, and very hardy. This need not be limiting with modern fabrics, but extra care should be taken in choosing them. Felt can be used in small quantities and should be shrunk by ironing it over a very damp cloth before you cut it. Felt will not machine wash, but if hand washed, it will spin dry.

8

What to stuff the toy with

Stuffing for toys can be home-made: cut up material, cut up clean nylon stockings (not the feet or tops). These are washable, but in the case of stockings, it takes a lot for one toy and the result is often lumpy and rather heavy. If the stuffing is dark in colour, it may show through light materials.

Kapok gives an excellent soft filling and is easy to stuff into toys. It is almost white and does not show through light materials, but it does not wash at all successfully. You can also use mill puff, which is used to fill very cheap pillows, and if more than one toy is anticipated, this works out cheaper than buying small bags of stuffing. It is cotton waste and is not quite as fine as kapok and has little bits of seed shell in it, but otherwise it is very good.

Foam is slightly more difficult to stuff into toys and does not give such a smooth finish as kapok, but it is excellent for washing. If you choose a light coloured one, it will not show through lighter fabrics. It is also very light in weight, a thought for large toys. Like mill puff, you can buy very cheap pillows filled with foam pieces, and for more than one toy this is cheaper than small bags.

Other fillers include nylon, Terylene, and other synthetics, but these, though excellent and washable, are not readily available.

Finishing materials

Other materials you will need are items for finishing: wools for hair, embroidery cottons for features, felts, braids, buttons and ribbon. These will often have to be bought, but one purchase often covers several toys.

Useful tools

You will find it useful to have these simple items to hand before you begin:

Cartridge (drawing) paper or brown paper for making patterns.
Ruler for marking grid for pattern.
Compass with a soft pencil.
Set square or piece of board with right-angle.
Soft pencil for marking paper patterns and marking in details
  on pattern.

Tailor's chalk for marking details on to material.
Scissors for cutting out.
Small scissors with sharp points for clipping between close
   stitching.
Assorted sewing cottons.
Assorted sewing needles, including a long upholstery needle
   and a leather needle which makes sewing on hair much
   easier. These can often be bought with a mattress needle
   together on a card.
Tape-measure.
Blunt knitting needle for working stuffing into difficult corners.

Preparing your pattern

The patterns at the back of the book are given on a squared
grid. The size of these squares can be varied to give toys of
different sizes. The sizes of the toys made in this book are
worked on a 1″ grid.

Start with a sheet of cartridge
or brown paper, and using
a ruler and set square or a
piece of board with a right angle,
draw a number of horizontal lines
spaced ½″, 1″ or 2″ apart.
Cross these with vertical
lines similarly spaced, thus
forming squares.
   Carefully copy a pattern
from the book, working from
square to square. Mark on to the
outline any relevant detail.
Cut out.
   This pattern gives you
the stitching line; no turnings
are allowed for. Mark on
the pattern piece what it is and
how many you should cut.

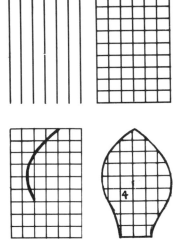

Cutting out

Pin pattern on material
and cut out as many pieces as
are required, adding ⅝"
for turnings. Mark joining marks
and top stitching lines.
Difficult details can be marked
on the material with soft pencil
or tailor's chalk by drawing
around the edge of the pattern.
Individual details are given
under each toy described
later in this book.

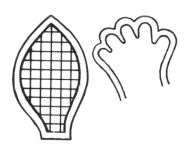

Making up the toy

Pin pieces together and tack
and stitch, carefully matching
seams and join marks. Sew
⅝" from edge of material.
Sew extra carefully around
fingers, etc., making sure
you follow the stitch line and
leaving enough room between
for cutting. Clip all inside curves
to avoid puckering.

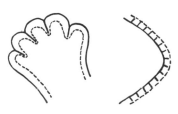

Turn pieces carefully to the right side and work into all
the difficult points with a blunt knitting needle.

Stuff each piece carefully, using small pieces of stuffing
and pressing them in evenly and tightly as you work to avoid
a lumpy effect. Join items together with even stitches, using
double cotton or button thread. In the case of joining heads to
bodies, work in extra stuffing at the neck as you stitch.

When joining on arms and legs, ears, wings, feet, etc.,
make sure that they are in a natural position and indicate the
character of the toy.

Adding features

It is when you add the features to a toy that it really comes
to life and becomes a personality. Spend time experimenting
with circles of felt and pieces of wool, moving them about
and seeing the effect before fixing them in place. Details of

11

features for the toys in this book are given under their separate headings.

Adding hair
The hair of a toy helps
to indicate its character,
age and nationality.

Short curly hair
Thread thick needle with
double length of wool and,
working in all directions,
make loops 1″ long over hair area
of head, joining in new lengths
as required. Trim odd ends.

Short straight hair, with fringe (bang)
Cut ½ oz. of wool into 12″
lengths and divide into two
bundles.

Thread needle with long length
of wool and, using first bundle,
fasten four strands at a time
at centre of wool along centre
parting with back stitch,
until the whole bundle has been
used. Now, taking two strands
at a time, back stitch in a
half circle 2″ from centre
parting, distributing the wool
evenly to cover the head.

Using second bundle of wool,
repeat stitching along centre
parting only, on top of first layer.
Trim hair to equal length
all round.

Fringes (bangs) Knot short
lengths of wool along side seam
on top of head and trim ends
evenly as fringe.

Four plaits or braids

Mark hair area into four equal
parts with tailor's chalk.
Thread needle with long length
of wool. Stitch from line to centre
of each area loosely until area
is covered.

When all areas are covered,
make up four small plaits
and stitch them to the centre
of each area. Tie ends
with a bow.

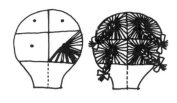

Two plaits (braids)

Mark hair area into two equal
halves down centre parting.
Thread needle with length of wool
and stitch very loosely
from centre parting to point
on side seam where there would
be an ear. When both sides
have been covered, make two
long or short plaits and stitch
to ears. Tie ends with a bow.

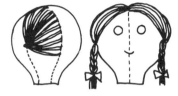

Details for long straight hair
are given under Alice on page 28.
Bald head as for clown
on page 38.

Clothes

It is not until the toy is made that you can make the clothes
for it. You would not make a dress for a child without
measuring the child. Here it is the same. Measure the toy
to check that the patterns given in this book will fit it.
Variations in size can happen, often because different
materials stretch or the stuffing varies. Follow all previous
instructions for drawing up patterns and cutting out.

Choice of materials

Use heavy materials for simple garments such as jackets,

14

light materials for other clothes. Hats and shoes are made from felt, or leather if available, socks and trousers from cotton interlock (jersey). Detailed suggestions are given under headings for individual toys.

Design your own toy

The patterns in this book can easily be adapted to provide more individual toys. Perhaps you want your doll tall and thin, to follow a family characteristic. Most patterns can be lengthened or shortened much as you would a dress pattern. Suggestions are given at the end of many of the individual patterns for adaptations, and for further toys that have broadly similar characteristics. In the case of dolls, a great variety can be achieved by changing colour of skin, colour and style of hair, colour of eyes and, of course, dress. Often to create a character from a favourite book or nursery rhyme it is only necessary to provide a variation of costume and colour.

Simple bear

Suggested materials
Nylon fur fabric, fur fabric, coating with a long pile, velvet, corduroy or chenille. Felt, leather or cotton materials for pads. Buttons for eyes.

Size in 1" pattern, 10½" high.

Using paper squared to 1", mark and cut out pattern number 1.

Lay pattern pieces on to material, direction of pile to run from top to bottom of bear. Cut out, allowing ⅝" turnings on pieces.

With right sides together, tack front and back bodies and nose. Stitch, leaving opening at side of bear for stuffing. Clip all inside curves and between ears and head, head and arms, arms and body, and between legs. Turn all pieces to right side and brush pile out of stitching.

Stuff body and nose not too firmly. Close side opening. Using double thread, run a gathering thread around neck and draw up slightly. Finish off well. Run a gathering thread on front of ears only and draw up slightly.

Using double thread, stitch through both thicknesses at arms and legs to make hinge.

Features
Sew nose to front of face with double thread, working around nose twice. Fasten off.
Eyes, sew on two small dark buttons.
Nose, sew a small triangle of leather or felt to nose.
Mouth, with embroidery cotton sew on shape of mouth.
Pads, from leather or felt cut out pads with no turnings allowed. Sew to flat of hands and base of feet. Mark in toes with embroidery thread.

Finish with a bow if liked.

Bear or panda

Suggested materials
Nylon fur fabric, fur fabric, coating with long pile, velvet, chenille or corduroy, in black and white for panda and any shade of gold or brown for bear. Felt or leather for pads, glass eyes or buttons, black felt for eye patches on panda.

Size in 1" pattern, 18" high.

Using paper squared to 1", mark and cut out pattern number 2.

Lay pattern pieces on material, direction of pile to run from top to bottom of items; panda is in two colours, head, nose and body white, ears, arms and legs black.

Cut out, allowing $\frac{5}{8}$" turning on all pieces.

With right sides together, tack front and back seams of head and body. Stitch front to back of head, two arms, two legs, two bodies, nose and two ears, leaving tops open for stuffing. Clip all inside curves and turn pieces to right side. If the fabric has a long pile, brush hair out from stitching around seams.

Stuff head. If you are using glass eyes, set them in position and twist them well together on the wrong side. Stuff body and attach head to body with double button thread, taking in $\frac{5}{8}$" on both items. Work round the head twice and fasten off.

Stuff nose and turn in $\frac{5}{8}$"
at open edge. Sew to face
with button thread, matching
seams. Work around nose
twice for firmness and fasten off.
Run a gathering thread $\frac{1}{4}$"
from edge of ears and draw up
to half original width.
Tuck up $\frac{5}{8}$" all round edge
of ear to the wrong side,
and shape ear by cupping it
over your thumb. Sew it to head
in a curve, the back of the ear
on side seam of head,

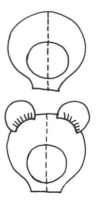

the front of the ear slightly
to the front.

Stuff arms and legs and sew up
openings, turning in ⅝".
From leather or felt
cut out pads with no turning
allowed. Sew to hands and feet,
and mark divisions for toes
with embroidery cotton.

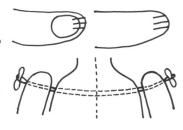

From scraps of leather or felt,
cut four strips 1½" x ½" and,
using these on the outside
of arms and legs to prevent
the thread pulling through,
sew arms and legs to body using
a long needle and several
thicknesses of button thread.
Pull up tightly. Work backwards
and forwards through limbs
and body at least four times.

Features
Nose, from black felt or
leather cut an oval 1" x ¾"
and sew on to nose, stuffing
behind very slightly.
Mouth, using embroidery thread,
mark in mouth in back stitch.
Panda eye-patches, cut felt
eye-patches and sew to head
close to nose.
Eyes, if glass eyes have not
already been added, sew on
black coat buttons for eyes.
Finish by adding bow to neck
with a yard of ribbon.

Further suggestions
Make up Goldilocks
(using Alice doll) and
three bears, one using
1" squares, one ¾" squares
and one ½" squares.

Mouse

Suggested materials

Velvet, corduroy, fur fabric, floral cotton, pink lining for ears, wool for tail, buttons for eyes, button thread for whiskers, embroidery cotton for nose.

Size in 1″ pattern, 11″ minus tail.

Using paper squared to 1″, mark and cut out pattern number 3.

Lay pattern pieces on material and cut out, allowing ⅝″ on all sides for turnings. Direction of pile to run from head to tail.

With right sides together, tack bodies together. Stitch, leaving opening at tail for stuffing. Turn to right side. Stuff, and sew up opening.

Features

Ears, using one piece of main body fabric and one of lining, tack ears and stitch. Turn to right side and press very lightly. Turn up ⅝″ on open end and attach to head, using a pleat to shape ear.

Eyes, sew on trouser buttons for eyes with button thread. Sew through head, drawing up slightly.

Nose, with pink embroidery cotton, embroider on a nose.

Whiskers, using button thread make whiskers by knotting 3″ lengths into nose on either side.

Tail, using several thicknesses of wool, plait (braid) a tail and stitch to end of mouse.

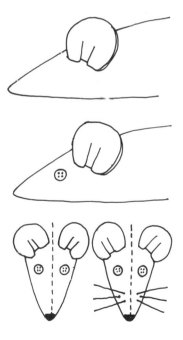

See photograph on page 53.

Baby doll

Suggested materials
Doll, skin coloured cotton, Winceyette.
Clothes, assorted materials, thin wool, cotton print, etc.
Wool for hair, felt for eyes, embroidery cotton for mouth,
felt or leather for shoes.

Size in 1″ pattern, 18″ high.

Using paper squared to 1″, mark and cut out pattern
number 4.
   Lay pattern pieces on material. Cut out, allowing ⅝″
turnings on all pieces. Mark with tailor's chalk or soft pencil

detail of hand, by drawing round pattern on wrong side of material.

With right sides together, tack front face to sides, matching cheeks. Stitch. Tack back head seam, and stitch. Tack front to back head, and stitch. Tack and stitch arms, legs and body, leaving tops open for stuffing and paying particular attention to fingers. Clip all inside curves and between fingers. Turn all pieces to right side.

Stuff all pieces, taking particular care to work stuffing well into fingers. Stuff firmly.

Stitch head on to body with double thread, taking in ⅝″ and, matching seams, work twice around neck for firmness. Fasten off.

Turn in ⅝″ to wrong side at top of arms and legs, and catch stitch opening closed with the seams at the side on arms and at the centre on legs.

With double thread, stitch arms to shoulders slightly to front of side body seam; stitch legs to base of body in the same way.

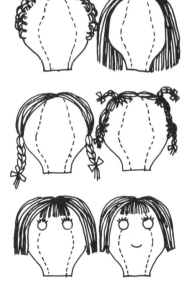

Hair, can be short and curly, long and straight, plaited in the English or African way, or short and straight. Choose which suits your doll and its nationality. Details of short curly, short straight, and two or four plaits (braids) are found on pages 12-13, long hair as for Alice on page 30.

Features

Eyes, cut two ½″ circles from felt of suitable colour and sew on to face with matching thread. Using dark cotton, stitch five ⅛″ long eye lashes at top of eye.

Mouth, with a soft pencil draw in mouth and embroider in pink embroidery cotton.

25

Clothes

English doll, using squared paper, mark and cut out dress and panties, petticoat, socks and shoes as patterns number 4 and 5.

Lay pattern on materials and cut out, allowing ⅝″ for seams.

Petticoat and panties, make up, joining shoulder and side seams on petticoat and side and leg seams on panties. Clip all inside curves and press all seams open. Trim neck, armholes, hem of petticoat and legs of panties with narrow lace. Make hem at top of panties and thread with elastic.

Dress, join shoulder and underarm seams of bodice; clip underarm seam and press seams open. Gather top of skirt to fit bodice and sew to bodice with ⅝″ turning. Sew back seam of skirt to within 2″ of bodice; press seam open. Neaten back opening by turning ⅝″ on both sides to wrong side of bodice and making a hem. Fasten with press studs (snaps). Make ¼″ hems at arm and neck edge with double cotton and draw up slightly. Turn up 1″ hem at lower edge.

Make a sash from remaining material or ribbon, and tie.

Socks, stitch ⅝″ from edge all the way around. Trim to ¼″ and turn to right side.

Shoes, from white felt cut four pieces as pattern with no seam allowance. Stitch ⅛″ from edge around foot; turn to right side and fasten with a bow.

Chinese doll (see photograph on page 36), using squared paper, mark and cut out dress and panties, petticoat, socks and shoes as patterns number 4 and 5.

Petticoat and panties, make up as for English doll.

Dress, join shoulder seams and underarm seams to marks. Clip underarm seams and press open.

Fold collar in half lengthways and stitch across either end. Turn in ¼″ hem on wrong side of both edges of diagonal opening. Stitch collar to neck edge to meet at centre front.

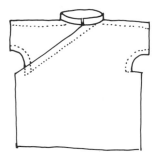

Turn in ¼" hem on wrong side at armhole edge and around lower skirt. Fasten diagonal opening and left side opening with press studs (snaps), leaving bottom free as on right side.

Make up socks and shoes as for English doll.

African doll (see photograph on page 36), using squared paper, mark and cut out panties in pattern number 5.
Panties, make up as for English doll.
Dress, hem ¼" all round length of material 12" x 6". Thread elastic through top hem and draw up to fit around underarms and overlap 3". Fasten overlap at top with press studs (snaps). Sew on shoulder straps of same material or ribbon. Make up necklace of shells or beads.

Doll

Alice through the looking glass

Suggested materials
Body, cotton, Winceyette, stockinette (jersey) in any flesh colour.
Dress, various materials. Alice's dress should be in a popular Victorian material: velvet, crepe, fine wool, striped cotton.
Apron, white cotton, gingham, broderie anglaise, muslin. Felt for shoes and eyes, stockinette (cotton jersey) for long socks, wool for hair, embroidery cotton for mouth.

Size in 1″ pattern, 18″ high.

Using paper squared to 1″, mark and cut out pattern number 6.
Lay pattern pieces on to material and cut out, allowing $\frac{5}{8}$″ for turnings on all pieces. Mark with tailor's chalk or soft pencil detail of hand, by drawing around hand on to the wrong side of the material.
With right sides together, tack front and back face seams. Stitch. Tack front to back head, matching seams, and stitch, leaving neck open. Tack and stitch arms, legs and body, leaving tops open for stuffing. Clip inside curves and between thumb and hand carefully. Turn all pieces to right side.
Stuff all pieces, taking particular care to work stuffing well into thumb and hand. Stuff firmly.
Stitch head on to body with double thread, taking in $\frac{5}{8}$″ and matching seams. Work twice around neck for firmness; fasten off.
Turn in $\frac{5}{8}$″ to wrong side at top of arms and legs and catch stitch opening closed. The seams should be at the side on arms and at centre on legs.
With double thread, stitch arms to shoulders slightly to the front side of the body seam. Stitch legs to base of body in the same way.

Hair, cut 1 oz. gold double knitting wool into 12″ lengths, retaining a small amount for sewing. Divide into two bundles. Thread needle with length of wool, and using first bundle fasten four strands at a time, at centre of wool, with back stitch to centre parting, until all the wool has been used. Now taking two strands at a time, sew in a half circle 2″ from centre parting, distributing wool evenly to cover head.

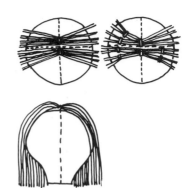

Using second bundle of wool, repeat stitching of centre parting only, on top of the first layer. Trim ends of hair even.

For other hair styles see pages 12-13.

Features

Eyes, cut two ½″ circles from blue felt and sew on to face with matching thread. Using dark brown cotton, stitch five ⅛″ long eyelashes at top of eye.

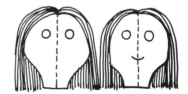

Mouth, with a soft pencil draw in mouth and embroider in pink embroidery cotton.

Clothes

Using squared paper, mark and cut out dress, panties, petticoat, socks, shoes and apron on pattern number 7.

Lay pattern pieces on to materials and cut out dress, panties, petticoat, socks and apron, allowing ⅝″ for seams.
Petticoat and panties, make up, joining shoulder and side seams on petticoat and side and leg seams on panties. Clip all inside curves and press all seams open.

Finish neck, armholes and hem of petticoat, and legs of

panties with narrow lace. Make hem at top of panties and thread with elastic.

Dress, join shoulder and underarm seams of bodice; clip underarm seam and press seams open. Gather top of skirt to fit bodice and sew to bodice, with $5/8''$ turning. Sew back seam of skirt to within $2''$ of bodice, and press seam open. Neaten back opening by turning $5/8''$ on both sides to wrong side of bodice and turning in a hem. Fasten with press studs (snaps).

Make $1/4''$ hems at arm and neck edge with double thread; draw up slightly and fasten off. Turn up $1''$ hem at bottom of skirt.

Apron, cut a long strip (or join two pieces of material together) to make a frill and make a narrow hem on one edge (this could be a length of broderie anglaise). Pleat the other edge of the strip and sew around edge of apron. Neaten. Finish neck edge with narrow hem. Make ties with $1'' \times 12''$ strips, hemmed on both sides. Sew to sides of apron. Sew on hook and eye at back of neck of apron.

Alice band, in same material as dress cut a strip $2''$ wide and $8''$ long. Fold in half along length, right sides together, and stitch $1/4''$ from edge. Turn to right side and press flat. Neaten ends and attach to a length of elastic to fit head.

Socks, stitch $5/8''$ from edge all the way around. Trim seam to $1/4''$ and turn to right side.

Shoes, from black felt cut four pieces as pattern with no seam allowance. Stitch $1/8''$ from the edge around foot. Turn to right side and fasten with a bow of wool.

Further suggestions
To make other dolls from this pattern.

Bride
Make a basic doll as for Alice, changing the hair style to one of those given in first chapter, pages 12-13, if desired. Make a dress using same pattern as Alice, with either long or short sleeves and long or short skirt.

Suggested material:
cotton curtain lace with
a scalloped edge, over a satin
petticoat. Buttons, bows and
ribbon as desired.

For a veil use a circle of net,
large or small, attached
to a coronet. This is a small circlet
of wire covered with lace,
flowers or ribbon.

The bouquet is a small
plastic doily with a hole cut
in the centre for small
plastic flowers; these could be
the same as for the headdress.
Neaten the back of the bouquet
with a length of ribbon.

Shoes should be white.

Try making a whole family.

Mother

Make a basic doll as for Alice,
changing the hair style
perhaps to a bun, as for the
Red Queen, in normal hair colour.

Make dress, using same
pattern as Alice with long sleeves
and long or short skirt in
cotton print, stripes or gingham.
Cover dress with apron,
made from a 6" x 6" square
gathered on one edge into
a length of material long enough
to tie round the waist.
Neaten edges.
Shoes as for Red Queen.

Father

Make up basic doll as clown,
with grey or brown hair,
a nose smaller and pink rather

32

than red, and no eye patches.
Make clothes as for clown,
in more suitable colours;
perhaps grey flannel jacket
and black and white striped
trousers in pillow ticking, with a
bright tie. Black shoes.

Baby

Make up basic Baby Doll
pattern to ¾" squared pattern.
For hair, make curls or plaits
(braids). Make clothes
as English Baby Doll,
using pretty light material.
Bright red shoes.

Try a really large doll,
approx 36" high.

Loopy Loo

Make up a basic doll
or Baby Doll using 2" squares
and thick, firm, cotton material
Stuff very firmly. Use thick wool
for hair which should be long
or in plaits (braids).
Dress as Alice in suitable
materials: cotton print or gingham,
with cotton apron, long or
short socks and black shoes.
(Don't forget to use 2" squares
for pattern.)

Attach loops of elastic under
sole of shoe so that a child can
slip them over her own feet
to make the doll walk.

Red Queen

Using red cotton material,
make up basic doll as for Alice.

Hair, using red wool, thread
a long length into needle and,
starting ½″ in front of the side
seam and following parting,
stitch loosely back and forth
to a line at nape of neck.
Work threads closely together,
and join in a new length
as required until both sides
of the head are covered.

   With a good quantity of wool
plait a fat plait (braid) 12″ long.
Fasten cut end and, working
from this end, coil it into a bun
at the nape of the Queen's neck,
stitching it in place as you coil.
Neaten end.

Features
Nose, using body material,
cut a 2″ circle. Gather it and stuff.
Fasten to centre of face.
Eyes, from black felt cut two
½″ circles and sew to face.
Stitch five ⅛″ eyelashes
at the top.
Mouth, with soft pencil mark a
straight mouth and embroider it
with dark red embroidery cotton.

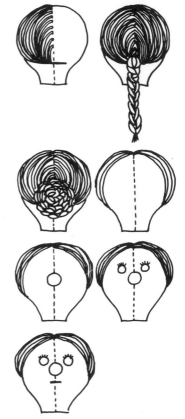

Clothes

Suggested materials
Dress, quilting, velvet, soft red wool or cotton.
Using paper squared to 1″, mark and cut out dress, crown and
shoes from pattern number 8.

Lay pattern for dress on material and cut out, allowing ⅝″ turnings on all pieces. Mark gather lines on material with tailor's chalk.

Join shoulder and underarm seams; clip underarm seam and press open. By machine or hand run double rows of gathering threads at top of skirt and on gather lines. Draw these up to make top of skirt fit bodice, then shape skirt to 16″, 20″, 24″. Stitch top of skirt to bodice ⅝″ from the edge. Stitch back seam of skirt to within 2″ of bodice. Press seam open. Neaten back opening by turning ⅝″ on either side to wrong side of bodice as a hem. Fasten with press studs (snaps). Make ¼″ hems at wrist and neck edge with double thread. Draw up slightly and fasten off. Turn up ¼″ hem at bottom of skirt.

Crown, using red felt cut out crown with no allowance for turnings. Allowing an ⅛″ seam, join points together on inner piece leaving back seam free.

Join outside piece to inner piece with outside piece on wrong side and ⅛″ seam. Turn outside piece to right side and top stitch ¼″ from lower edge. Close back seam.

Gather and stuff circle for knob and sew to top of crown.

Shoes, using red felt cut four pieces for shoes with no turnings allowed. Sew two together, stitching ⅛″ from edge and leaving 1″ open at front for lacing.

Turn to right side and lace with needle and wool.

Left:
Baby dolls, pages 24-27.
Alice through the looking glass, page 28.

Clown

Suggested materials

White cotton for upper body with a scrap of red material for nose. Corduroy, velvet, gingham, striped cotton, or plain coloured material for trousers. Heavy cotton, close woven wool, any material that is the same on both sides for jacket. Yellow and black felt for eyes, black felt for shoes, and scraps of felt for flower; wool for hair, embroidery cotton for mouth.

Size in 1″ pattern, 16″ high.

Using paper squared to 1″, mark and cut out body as pattern number 9.

Lay pattern pieces on to materials and cut out, allowing ⅝″ for turnings on all pieces. Mark with tailor's chalk or soft pencil detail of hand, by drawing around hand on wrong side of material.

With right sides together, tack front and back head seams and stitch. Tack front and back head and stitch. Join top to lower half at waist seams and press. Tack back and front centre seams and stitch to mark. Tack front and back bodies together and stitch, leaving neck open for stuffing. Tack arm pieces together and stitch, taking care around fingers. Clip all inside curves and between fingers. Turn all pieces to right side and stuff, working stuffing carefully into fingers and feet before stuffing arms and legs.

Stitch head on to body with double thread, taking in ⅝″ and matching seams; work twice around neck for firmness. Fasten off.

Turn in ⅝″ to wrong side at top of arms and stitch opening closed.

Join arms to body at shoulders, setting them slightly to front of side seams. Fasten off strongly.

Hair, using brightly coloured wool cut approximately $1/3$ oz. of double knitting wool into 6″ lengths. Place halfway down head, and starting $1/2$″ in front of the side seam, knot two strands at a time, in a line $1/2$″ apart, to $1/2$″ in front of side seam on other side. Work second row above first, working the knots in the spaces of the first row. Trim wool to an even length all round head.

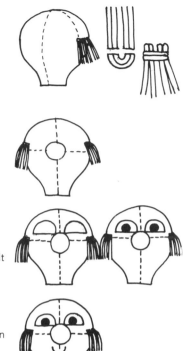

Features

Nose, gather a 3″ circle of red material. Draw up, stuff, and sew to centre of face.

Eyes, cut a 2″ circle of yellow felt and cut into two. Sew to face slightly above centre line and close to nose.

Cut two $1/2$″ circles of black felt and sew to eye shapes.

Mouth, with a soft pencil mark in mouth as a small half circle under nose. Embroider with red embroidery cotton.

Clothes

Using paper squared to 1″, mark and cut out pattern number 9 for jacket, bow tie, flower and shoes.

Lay pattern pieces on material and cut out jacket, allowing $5/8$″ for turnings on shoulders and underarm seams.

Cut out flower and shoes in felt with no turnings.

Jacket, join shoulder and underarm seams. Clip curve under arm and press seams open. Work blanket stitch in wool or embroidery cotton around front, bottom, back, neck and cuffs - or finish with braid or contrasting binding. Press lapels to right side.

Flower, take two flower shapes and place one over the other.

Cut a ¾″ circle of contrasting felt for centre. Place this in centre of flower and, working through all thicknesses, gather around circle and draw up slightly to raise centre. Sew to lapel of jacket.

Fit jacket on to clown and, lapping left over right, sew on two press studs (snaps) to fasten. Sew on four buttons to make jacket double-breasted.

Bowtie, using two lengths of material 2½″ wide and 8″ long, fold in half down length and stitch ¼″ from edge. Turn to right side and press. From one length cut off sufficient to go around neck and overlap 1″. Neaten ends. Using second length, fold ends to centre and stitch into a bow. Take a small piece of same material over centre to simulate knot. Stitch to one end of neck band and sew one half of a press stud underneath and the corresponding socket to other end of neck band. Fasten around neck of clown.

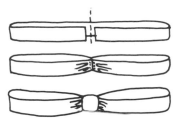

Boots, from black felt cut four pieces for boots with no allowance for turnings. Sew in twos, stitching ⅛″ from edge and leaving 1″ open at front for lacing.

Turn to right side and lace with needle and wool.

Tweedledum and Tweedledee

Using same pattern as clown, make up two basic dolls using pink for heads, hands and legs, and white for upper body.

Size in 1″ pattern, 16″ high.

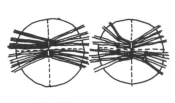

Hair, cut 1 oz. wool into 9″ lengths, leaving over small amount for sewing. Divide into four equal bundles, two for each doll.

Thread needle with length of wool and, using first bundle, fasten four strands at a time at centre of wool along centre parting with back stitch, until the whole bundle of wool has been used. Now taking two strands at a time, back stitch in a half circle 1″ from centre parting, distributing the wool to cover the head evenly.

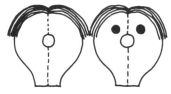

Using second bundle of wool, repeat stitching along centre parting only, on top of the first layer. Trim all ends evenly.

Features
Nose, cut a circle of dark pink cotton 2½″. Gather, stuff, and sew to centre of face.
Eyes, from brown felt cut two ½″ circles and sew to face.
Mouth, with a soft pencil mark in a mouth and embroider with pink embroidery cotton.

Clothes
Using paper squared to 1″, mark and cut out pattern number 9: jacket, collar, trousers, cap and shoes. Cut out and make up as clown.
Jacket, bind edges in contrasting colour to make a blazer.

Collar, cut four from white material and make up into two collars, binding neck edge. Attach short length of bright ribbon to either end to tie, and embroider DUM and DEE on left-hand corner in back stitch in same colour.

Trousers, cut from interlock (jersey) or stretch fabric if possible, in a light colour. Stitch front and back seam as far as mark, then side and leg seams. Turn ½″ hems at bottom of legs and top of trousers. Try on trousers and sew on ribbon as braces, crossing them at the back.

Cap, from two colours of felt,
cut four pieces of side and side
front out of each colour,
and two pieces of peak in each
colour, allowing ¼″ for turnings
on all pieces.

Alternating contrasting colours, sew front seams and back seams with ¼" seams. Join on side pieces in the same way, then join front to back.

Make up peak by joining one piece of each colour ¼" from curved edge. Turn to right side and top stitch ¼" from edge. Place peak to front of cap, right sides together, and stitch. Turn up ¼" as a hem on wrong side at lower edge and top stitch. Cover a small button with a gathered circle of felt and sew to top of cap to neaten.

Shoes, from black felt cut four pieces from pattern with no seam allowance. Stitch ⅛" from the edge around foot, leaving 1" open at front for lacing. Turn to right side and lace with needle and wool.

Mermaid

Suggested materials
Upper body, shades of pale green or blue cotton; tail, fishy patterned material in greens and blues. Wool for hair, felt for shells and eyes.

Size in 1" pattern, 20" tall.

Use pattern of clown for upper body and pattern number 10 for tail. Cut out and make up mermaid, following clown and fish directions. Add shells to upper body as photograph, with small amount of stuffing behind. Add long hair, eyes and mouth as for Alice.

Humpty Dumpty

Suggested materials
Face, white, cream or light brown thick cotton with dark pink for nose.
Body, almost any material: corduroy, velvet, tartan, gingham, striped cotton, etc. Material for tie in contrast, or picking up one of the colours used for the body.

Buttons, wool for hair, felt for eyes and shoes, red embroidery cotton for mouth, and colour of hair for eyebrows.

Size in 1″ pattern, 18″ high.

Using paper squared to 1″, mark and cut out pattern number 11.

Lay main pattern pieces on materials and cut out, allowing $5/8$″ for turnings on all pieces. Mark stitching line for hands by drawing around pattern on wrong side of material with tailor's chalk.

With right sides together, tack face pieces to body pieces at waist. Stitch. Tack front and back seams, matching waist seams. Stitch. Tack front to back and stitch all the way round, leaving opening for stuffing at one side. Turn to right side and stuff firmly.

Tack hands to arms and stitch. Tack arms together, stitching carefully around fingers. Clip carefully between fingers and turn to right side, working into fingers with blunt knitting needle. Tack legs together and stitch.

Stuff arms and legs, paying particular attention to fingers and working stuffing into them with blunt needle. Turn in $5/8$″ at top of arms and legs, and slip stitch opening together. Sew arms to body with double thread, 1″ down from waist seam and to the front of side seam, with thumbs uppermost. Sew legs on either side of centre seam at bottom.

Tie, cut strip of material 3″ wide
and the length of the waist,
and a strip 3″ by 12″.
With right sides together,
fold in half in middle along length
and stitch $5/8$″ from edge.
Turn to right side and press.

Using long strip, join ends
at centre front of body,
placing it over waist seam.
Catch in place at side seams
and centre back.

Make bow from short strip
by joining ends to middle
and gathering up slightly.
Take a small scrap of same
material and fold over centre,
stitching to make a knot.
Sew resulting bow to centre of tie,
over join. Sew four buttons
to body.

Shoes, from black felt cut four
shoes with no turning allowed.
Stitch two pieces together
for each shoe, stitching $1/8''$
from edge and leaving $1''$ open
at front for lacing. Turn to
right side and lace shoes
with length of wool and needle.
Put on feet and tie with bow.

Features

Nose, from pink material cut a
$3''$ circle and gather $1/4''$
from edge. Stuff and draw up
gathers. Sew to centre of face.
Eyes, cut two $1''$ circles from felt
and sew to face.
Eyebrows and mouth, with soft
pencil mark eyebrows above
eyes, and mouth under nose.
Then, using embroidery thread,
mark them in in back stitch.
Hair, cut small amount of wool
into $6''$ lengths. Stitch this to top
of head with back stitch,
taking in 3 strands of wool
with each stitch. Start hair $1''$
in front of side seam. Trim ends
even.

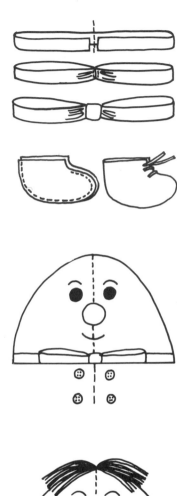

Further suggestions

Adapt this pattern to make
your own individual Gonk,
using mad fabrics.

Pop Star

Make up egg as Humpty Dumpty,
using pink for nead
and an outlandish material
for body. Hair should be thick
and long, trimmed evenly all round
in a pudding basin hair cut.
Make nose large and pink.
Add floppy bow tie,
and brass buttons.

Devil

Make up egg in bright red,
using Humpty Dumpty pattern.
Change feet into hooves and add
barbed tail and horns.
Add smart collar and tie and
large red buttons. Hair and face
as Humpty Dumpty,
using red and black only.

Baby

Make up egg as Humpty Dumpty,
using pink for face and body;
make back of head white
for bonnet. Add a curl of wool
to top of head. Sew a frill
of white lace or broderie anglaise
around side seam, and sew on
ribbon to either side and tie
under chin. Pin on nappy (diaper).

Dolly Rocker

Make up egg as for
Humpty Dumpty, using pink
for head and arms, white for body
and legs.

Hair, using thick wool 24″ long, knot at centre of wool in a circle around head and draw to top of head in a pony tail. Secure and finish with a bow.
Dress, gather a yard of heavy cotton lace 4″ wide and sew to waist seam. Neaten by belt of ribbon with bow at front. Sew narrow lace around join of leg to body.
Face, eyes and mouth as Humpty Dumpty, cheeks 1½″ circles of pink felt.

Clown

Make up egg as Humpty Dumpty, using white for head and hands and a strongly patterned or bright coloured fabric for body. Cut revers in felt and sew on to body. Make bow tie as Humpty Dumpty, face as clown on page 40.

Short hair as Humpty Dumpty.

Right:
Mouse, page 23.
Mermaid, page 46.

Cat

Suggested materials
Any material that is rich and 'catty': velvet, corduroy, wool,
satin, striped cotton, printed cotton, and fur fabric in any
cat colour or something really outlandish. Coloured felt for
eyes and nose, wool in matching body colour for tail, embroidery thread for mouth and whiskers.

Size in 1″ pattern, 12″ high.

Using paper squared to 1″, mark and cut out pattern
number 12.
    Lay pattern pieces on material. The direction of pile, if
any, should run from head to tail. Cut out, allowing ⅝″
turnings on all pieces. Mark stitching line for feet by drawing
around pattern on wrong side of material with tailor's chalk.
    With right sides together, tack body pieces together. Stitch,
leaving opening for stuffing at tail end. Tack legs together
and stitch, taking care around toes. Clip all inside curves
and between toes. Turn body and legs to right side.
    Stuff body, not too firmly, and sew up opening. Stuff legs
lightly, working stuffing well into toes. Turn in ⅝″ to wrong
side at top of legs and catch stitch together. Sew to front
of body as indicated.

Tail, plait (braid) several
thicknesses of matching
wool 12″ long and sew
to centre bottom of body.
Add bow if fancied.

Features
Eyes, cut two lozenges 1½″
by 1″ from gold, green
or grey felt and sew to body.
Mark pupil on centre of eye
with embroidery cotton,
in satin stitch.
Nose, cut triangle 1″ by 1″
by 1″ from pink felt
and sew on as nose.

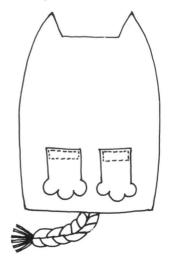

Mouth, mark mouth shape on to face with soft pencil or tailor's chalk and mark in with back stitch in embroidery cotton.

Whiskers, mark three lines for whiskers on face and embroider in back stitch.

Further suggestions

Following similar methods, design your own flat animals.

Dog

Any doggy material can be used. Use cat pattern but omit ears from head. Cut ears from main fabric and lining, and attach at the top of head to hang down.

Eyes should be black on white circles. Nose, rectangle of felt. Tail plaited (braided), but much shorter than cat's.

Rabbit

Rabbit coloured material or fluffy white material, corduroy, etc.

Make using cat pattern omitting ears and making body longer. Ears should be long, lined with pink and stiffened. Attach to top of head so that they stand up straight. Eyes are circles of felt, nose a pink triangle, and tail a white pom pom. Feet as cat's, but sewn higher on body.

Kangaroo

Brown materials. Use cat pattern but omit ears from head. Cut fairly small ears separately

and attach to top of head
to stand up straight. Eyes are
black on white circles,
nose a triangle of felt.
Attach long tail in same material
at bottom. Feet as cat's but sewn
higher on body.
Joey is a small version of adult
popped into a pocket stitched
to front of mother.

Elephant
Soft grey materials or 'pink'.
Make as cat, but omit ears
and round off top of head.
Ears are large ovals
lined with pink, gathered
on one side and attached
at sides of head. Eyes are small
black circles. Legs are straight,
with half circles of white.
Trunk is narrow tube of
same material stuffed lightly
and attached to face. Tusks are
white felt, sewn either side
of trunk. Tail is a thin grey plait
(braid).

Frog or toad

Suggested materials
Upper body, printed cotton with free spot design in greens and brown, velvet, corduroy, satin or damask in shades of green or brown.
Underparts, lighter tone of upper body colour in plain fabric. Yellow and black felt for eyes.

Size in 1″ pattern, 13″ from bottom to nose, 20″ from back foot to back foot.

Using paper squared to 1″, mark and cut out pattern number 13.
Lay pattern pieces on two materials, matching pattern if any. Cut out, allowing ⅝″ for turnings on all pieces.
With right sides together, tack top of body to top of sides of body, matching eyebrows and joining to a point at nose. Stitch. Again with right sides together, tack top of body to underbody, carefully matching head, legs and feet. Stitch, leaving opening at back for stuffing. Clip all inside curves and turn to right side, working into all the corners with a blunt knitting needle. Press feet flat.
Mark toe line from pattern on to feet with tailor's chalk or soft pencil and top stitch.
Stuff, starting with the feet and working stuffing carefully into toes, legs, then head (working stuffing into eyebrows) and finally body. Sew up opening, working further stuffing in as you stitch.

Features
Eyes, cut two circles of yellow felt 1½″ in diameter and two lozenges of black felt 1¼″ by 1″. Sew black lozenges in centre of yellow circles.
Sew eyes to frog's head under eyebrow, working in a small amount of stuffing behind eyes as you stitch, to make them protrude.

Crocodile

Suggested materials
Upper body, printed cotton simulating scales in green or brown, velvet, corduroy, or cotton in green or brown.
Underparts, lighter tone of upper body colour in plain fabric.
Mouth, red cotton, yellow and black felt for eyes, white felt for teeth.

Size in 1" pattern, 23" long.

Using paper squared to 1", mark and cut out pattern number 14.

Lay pattern pieces on three materials, matching pattern if any. Cut out, allowing $\frac{5}{8}$" for turnings on all pieces.

With right sides together, tack under body to top side body pieces, matching feet. Stitch, taking care around toes. Tack and stitch top body to top side body, matching eyebrows and leaving opening on one side for stuffing. Set in mouth piece carefully. Tack and stitch.

Clip all inside curves between toes. Turn to right side, and work into all the corners with a blunt knitting needle.

Cut a piece of stiffening for mouth, using thick paper or cardboard. Using mouth pattern piece with no turnings, fold in half and slip into mouth on inside of crocodile.

Stuff, starting with the head, then feet and legs, working stuffing well into toes. Stuff main body and tail firmly. Sew up opening.

Features
Eyes, cut two circles of yellow felt $1\frac{1}{2}$" in diameter and two lozenges of black felt $1\frac{1}{4}$" by 1". Sew black lozenges to centre of yellow circles. Sew eyes to crocodile's eyebrows, working in a small amount of stuffing behind the eyes as you stitch to make them protrude.
Teeth, cut a strip of white felt 12" by $\frac{1}{2}$" and cut in a narrow zigzag down centre. Sew half to upper jaw and half to lower jaw as teeth.

61

Dachshund

Suggested materials

Almost any fabric: wool, cotton, velvet, bouclé, fur fabrics; lining for inside ear. Trouser buttons for eyes, matching wool for tail, short length of leather or plastic binding or ribbon for collar, fastened with very small buckle or button.

Size in 1" pattern, 19" minus tail.

Using paper squared to 1", mark and cut out pattern number 15.

Lay pattern pieces on material, and if fabric has pile, this should run from head to tail. Cut out, allowing ⅝" turnings on all pieces. From lining cut under-ears. Mark stitching line for feet by drawing round pattern on wrong side of material with tailor's chalk or soft pencil.

With right sides together, tack two body pieces together and stitch, leaving opening at tail for stuffing. Tack legs and stitch carefully around toes. Tack and stitch ears, leaving top open. Clip all inside curves and carefully between toes, and turn all pieces to right side. Press ears.

Stuff body very firmly and sew up opening. Stuff legs rather lightly, and turn in ⅝" at top and catch stitch together. Sew to body with double thread as marked on pattern.

Features

Ears, turn in ⅝″ to wrong side
of ear and pleat underside of ear.
Stitch to head as marked
on pattern so that ears have
an intelligent lift.

Nose, cut a 1″ diameter circle
from black felt or leather
and sew to end of nose,
gathering it slightly.

Eyes, sew on black trouser
buttons with button thread,
stitching through head and
drawing up slightly.

Tail, plait (braid) several
thicknesses of matching wool
18″ long, and sew on to body.

Collar, from bright coloured
leather, plastic or ribbon,
cut a sufficient length
to go around dog's neck
and fasten with small buckle
or button.

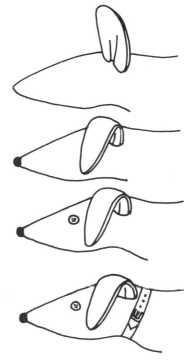

Hen and chicks

Hen

Suggested materials
Body, patterned cotton simulating feathers, or plain coloured cotton in shades of copper, grey, white or black. Yellow cotton for beak and red for comb and wattles. Yellow or matching shade of wool for tail and wing feathers, and yellow wool for legs. Felt in white and black for eyes and thin foam rubber sheet or padding for wings.

Size in 1″ pattern, 16″ long.

Using paper squared to 1″, mark and cut out pattern number 16.
   Lay pattern pieces on material, watching direction of pattern, if any. Cut out, allowing ⅝″ for turnings on all pieces.

With right sides together, tack beak to body pieces and stitch. Press open seam.
   With right sides together, tack comb and wattle pieces together leaving tops open. Stitch. Clip between scallops of comb and turn all pieces to right side and press flat. Pleat wattles and tack pleat. Tack wattles to the right side of the sides of the hen, following marks.
   Tack comb to one of the sides in similar manner, easing it into the shape of the curve and tacking down scallops to keep them out of the way.

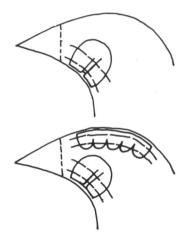

See photograph on page 72.

64

With right sides together, tack under-body to sides, fitting it from beak to tail. Stitch. Match curves and tack around beak and over head and back to tail. Stitch, leaving tail open for stuffing. Clip all inside curves and turn to right side. Release tacking threads holding comb and wattles.

Stuff, working stuffing carefully into beak before starting on body. Stuff firmly and sew up opening at tail flat.

Cut two wing shapes from padding or foam sheet.

With right sides together, tack wings together in pairs with padding or foam on the outside. Stitch, leaving end of wing open. Turn to right side and press lightly. Sew up opening, turning in $5/8''$ to wrong side. Sew wings on to body as indicated with strong thread.

Feathers, using a double thickness of wool, work loops about 1″ long over closed openings at tail and wings.

Features

Eyes, cut out eye shapes in white and black felt. Stitch black circles to right and left-hand sides of white ovals. Sew these to either side of head.

Legs, twist several thicknesses of yellow wool 36″ long tightly and, doubling wool back on itself, twist into shape of hen's foot. Toes should be approximately $2\frac{1}{2}''$ long. Catch wool with a stitch where toes join. Fasten leg end of wool tightly, to stop it unwinding, and join to body under wings. Catch leg at base seam and fix the foot in a sitting position.

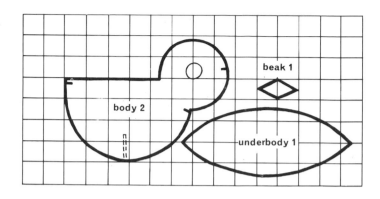

Chicks

Suggested materials

Brushed Acrilan or Courtelle, fluffy yellow wool, or plain cotton or Winceyette. Yellow wool for tail and legs, yellow felt for beak, black felt for eyes.

Size in 1", pattern 7" long.

Using paper squared to 1", mark and cut out pattern number 17.

Lay pattern pieces on material (quantity of chicks un-restricted). Cut out, allowing $5/8''$ for turnings on all pieces.

With right sides together, tack underbody to sides. Stitch. Tack head and back together. Stitch, leaving an opening at tail for stuffing. Turn to right side and stuff. Sew up opening. Make loops for tail in yellow wool over closed opening. Using short length of wool and only double thickness, make legs as for hen and sew to body at side.

Features

Beak, cut beak in felt.
Fold in half at centre
and sew to front of head.
Eyes, cut two circles in black felt
$1/4''$ in diameter and sew
to either side of head.

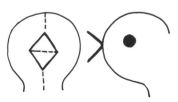

Fish

Suggested materials
Almost any material: plain and printed cotton, gingham, velvet and satin. Felt in two colours for eyes, rick rack braid for fins.

Size in 1″ pattern, 18″ long.

Using paper squared to 1″, mark and cut out pattern number 18.
  Lay pattern pieces on materials and cut out, allowing ⅝″ for turnings on all pieces.
  With right sides together, tack faces to bodies. Stitch. Tack bodies together and stitch, leaving opening at tail for stuffing. Tack and stitch tailpieces together. Clip into mouth and V of tail, and turn both pieces to right side and press flat.
  Stuff body and tail, not too firmly, and join tail into body to close gap.

Features
Eyes, cut two circles 2″ in diameter and two 1″ in diameter from felt. Sew the smaller onto the centre of the larger with embroidery thread. Sew eyes to either side of face.
Fins, catch stitch rick rack braid to back and underside of fish, following seam.

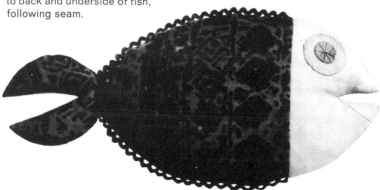

Pig

Suggested materials
Strong cotton or leather. Buttons for eyes, felt for nostrils, ring for nose.

Size in 1″ pattern, 14″ long.

Using paper squared to 1″, mark and cut out pattern number 19.

Lay pattern pieces on material and cut out, allowing ⅝″ on all sides for turnings.

With right sides together, tack under-body to two side bodies, matching legs. Stitch. Tack top seam of body and stitch, leaving opening at tail for stuffing. Set in nose piece carefully. Tack and stitch.

Clip all inside curves and between toes. Turn to right side and stuff firmly, paying special attention to legs. Sew up opening.

Features
Ears, tack ear pieces together and stitch. Turn to the right side and press. Turn up ⅝″ at top edge and attach to head using a pleat to shape ear.
Eyes, sew on trouser buttons for eyes with button thread. Sew them together and draw up slightly through the head.
Nose, cut two ½″ circles from felt and sew to nose as nostrils. Attach a curtain ring between the nostrils for a ring.
Tail, fold tail in half lengthways and stitch. Run a gathering thread with double cotton close to stitching within the seam. Leave needle attached.
Turn tail to right side, drawing up gathering thread until tail curls, and sew to pig.

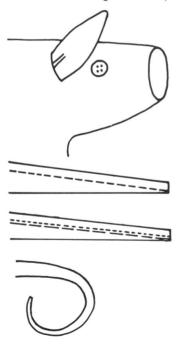

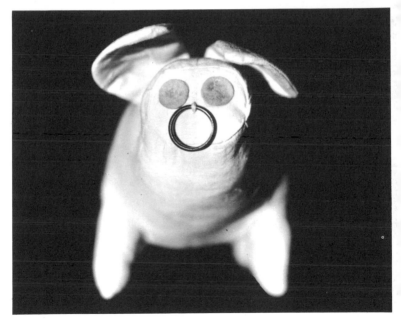

69

Hobby horse

Suggested materials
Head, strong heavy material: furnishing (upholstery) velvet, fur fabric, corduroy, furnishing cotton. Use a contrast to line ears. 1½ yards leather or plastic binding for reins and harness, 1″ wide. 2 oz. wool for mane and tail. Black buttons for eyes, bells, wooden frame.

Size of head in 1″ pattern.

Make up frame as drawing on page 74 or 75.
Using paper squared to 1″, mark and cut out pattern number 20.
Lay pattern pieces on material and cut out, allowing ⅝″ on all sides for turnings. Direction of pile if any to run from front to back.
With right sides together, tack two heads together and stitch, leaving neck open. Clip all inside curves and turn to right side. Slip head over frame head and stuff carefully, working stuffing evenly on both sides of frame and between frame and seam line. If you bind strips of foam rubber around frame head before fitting material head over it, this makes further stuffing easier.
Turn up ⅝″ at neck end of head and, using several thicknesses of button thread, run a gathering thread on fold. Draw up tightly, working extra stuffing in as you draw up to make neck really firm. Fasten off very thoroughly.

Features
Ears, using one main body fabric ear and one lining, tack ears together and stitch. Turn to right side and press lightly.
Turn up ⅝″ on open end and attach to head, using a pleat to shape ear.
Eyes, sew on coat buttons for eyes with button thread.

Mane, using 12″ lengths of wool, two at a time, knot down back seam starting 2″ in front of ear and ending 2″ from end of neck.

Harness, from 1½ yards of leather or plastic binding, cut 1 yard. Fold in half through centre and stitch for reins. Cut the remainder through the centre and follow drawing for placing of harness and reins. Stitch through all thicknesses in star pattern to secure. Add bells to mouth on loops of thread.

Tail, cut remainder of wool into 36″ lengths and tie at centre. Glue into hole on frame, pushing wool in, or bind on to frame with length of wool using glue to hold.

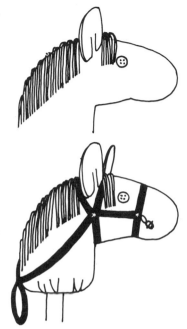

Left:
Hen and chicks, see pages 64-6.
Crocodile, page 60. Frog, page 58.

Frame 1

Following diagram, cut head
in hardboard 1″ smaller round
than pattern, and 2″ shorter
in the neck.

In a 42″ length of 1¼″
dowel or broom handle, cut a
slot 6″ long to take head.
Drill ½″ diameter hole
at right angles to head slot,
12″ from top, and a hole
the size of the castor spindle
in the bottom end. Also
a shallow hole halfway down the
length of dowel to glue tail into.

Glue and pin head into slot.
Glue and pin 12″ by ½″ dowel
into hole for handles.
Hammer castor into hole
at bottom.

. Rub wood down and finish
with two coats
of sealer or varnish.

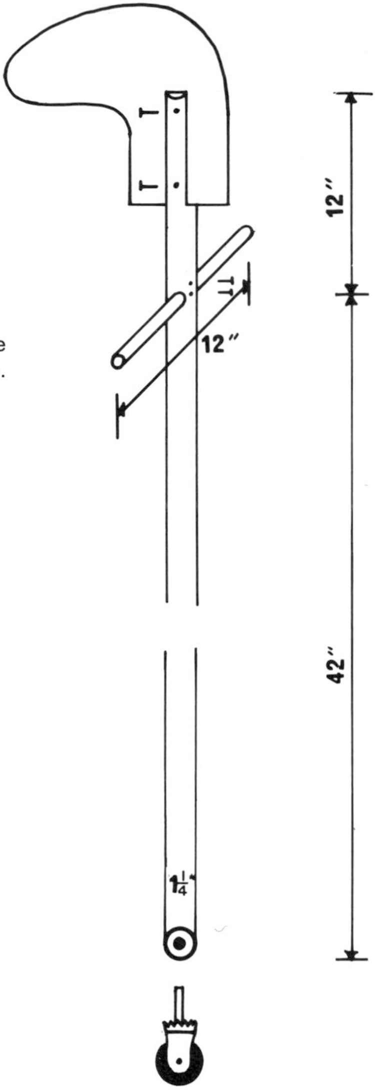

Frame 2

Following diagram, cut head
in hardboard 1″ smaller round
than pattern and 2″ shorter
in the neck.

In a 42″ length of 1″ by 1″
dowel cut a slot 6″ long to take
head. Drill ½″ diameter hole
at right angles to head slot,
12″ from top, and a hole
halfway down length for tail
to be glued in.

Make a mortice and tenon joint
with this upright piece
and the centre of the 12″ length
of 1″ by 1″ that is to take the
wheels.

Glue and pin head in slot.
Glue and pin 12″ length of
½″ dowel into hole for
handles. Glue and pin mortice
and tenon joint.

Screw wheels to centre
at either end of 12″ length,
so that they run freely.

Rub wood down, rounding
corners, and finish with
two coats of sealer or varnish.

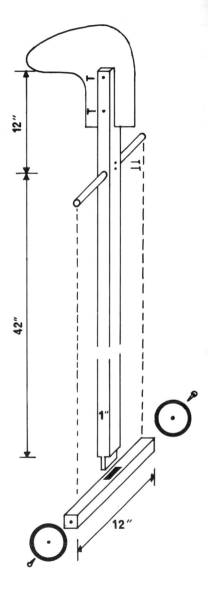

Horse, zebra or donkey

Suggested materials
Fur fabrics, velvet, pile fabrics, leather, wool, striped cotton, cotton, lining for ears. Wool for manes and tails, buttons for eyes, leather or plastic binding for harness.

Size in 1″ pattern, 12″ high.

Using paper squared to 1″, mark and cut out pattern number 21.
    Lay pattern pieces on material and cut out, allowing ⅝″ on all sides for turnings. Direction of pile to run from head to tail.

With right sides together, tack under-body to two side bodies, matching legs. Stitch. Tack head and top of body together and stitch, leaving opening at tail for stuffing. Clip all inside curves and turn to right side. Stuff firmly, paying special attention to legs. Sew up opening.

Features

Ears, using one main body fabric ear and one lining, tack ears and stitch. Turn to right side and press very lightly. Turn up $5/8''$ on open end and attach to head, using a pleat to shape ear.

Eyes, sew on trouser buttons for eyes with button thread. Sew through head, drawing up slightly.

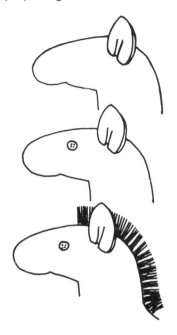

Mane, using 4″ lengths of wool, knot to neck on seam starting slightly to front of ears and continuing to curve where neck joins body. In the case of the zebra, follow black and white stripes and use these colours in wool alternately. For the horse, leave wool long, and for donkey and zebra cut hair to 1″ long.

Tail, donkey and zebra

Using several thicknesses of wool, plait (braid) 6″ length. Fasten off with wool and leave 1″ tassel. Sew to end of body.

Tail, horse

Using several thicknesses of wool 12″ long, fold in half, tie at fold, and sew to end of body.

Horse and donkey

Using thin strips of leather
or plastic, make harness
on small scale as for hobby horse.

Donkey

Cut hat from felt.
Stitch backseam and decorate
with flowers. Pannier baskets
are cut from felt, or you can use
cress baskets if you can
get them. Attach round middle
of donkey with wide strap of felt.

Hedgehog

Suggested materials
Upper body, long haired dark fabric, patterned cotton simulating quills.
Under body and face, smooth fabric in matching colour. Matching felt for ears and feet, trouser buttons for eyes.

Size in 1″ pattern, 9″ long.

Using paper squared to 1″, mark and cut out pattern number 22.

Lay pattern pieces on two materials, direction of hair to run from head to tail. Cut out, allowing ⅝″ turning on all pieces.

With right sides together, join right and left faces and bodies. Tack back seam and stitch. Tack upper body to under body, matching carefully at nose. Stitch, leaving gap at tail for stuffing. Brush hair out from stitching around seams. Turn to right side and stuff. Turning in ⅝″, sew up opening.

Feet, from felt cut eight feet without seam allowance and, using double thickness, sew together ⅛" from edge. Sew feet to under body in the position marked on the pattern.

Features
Ears, from felt cut one circle 1" in diameter and cut in half through middle, giving two half circles. Fold points to centre, and sew resulting ear to seam line.

Nose, cut a small triangle of black felt and sew on as nose over seam.

Eyes, sew on two black trouser buttons as eyes with button thread, connecting them through the head and drawing them up slightly. Finish off thread behind button.

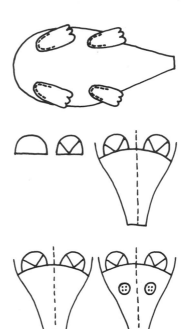

Patterns

1 Simple bear

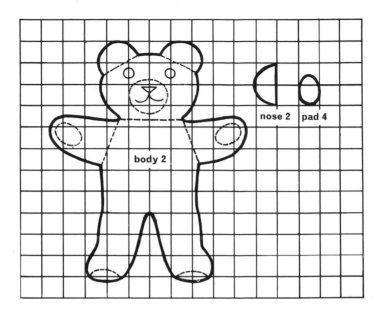

nose 2   pad 4

body 2

2 Bear or panda

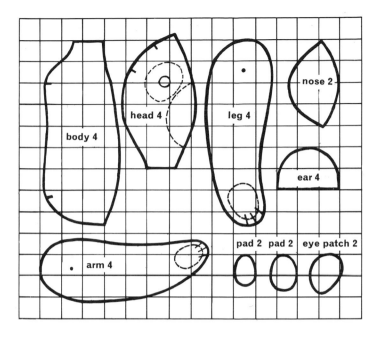

3 Mouse

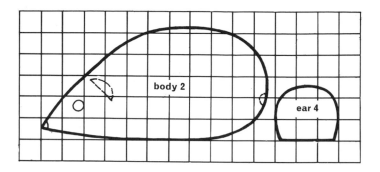

body 2

ear 4

4 Baby doll

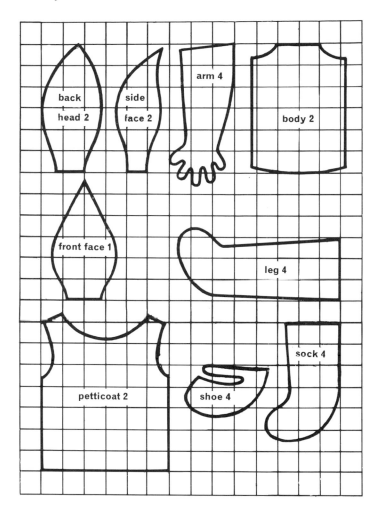

5 Baby doll, English and Chinese dress

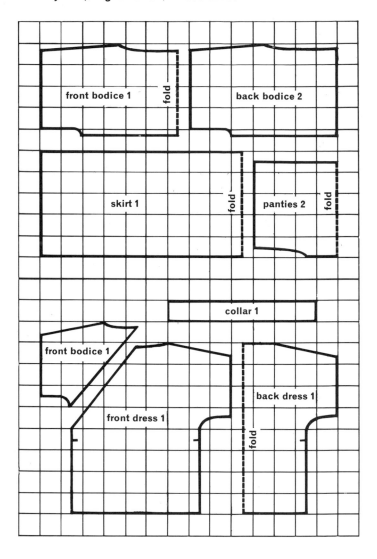

front bodice 1

fold

back bodice 2

skirt 1

fold

panties 2

fold

collar 1

front bodice 1

front dress 1

back dress 1

fold

6 Alice doll

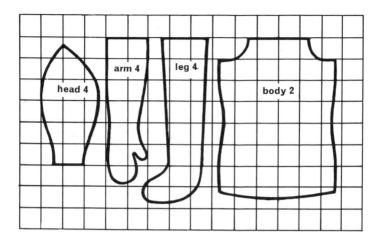

head 4

arm 4

leg 4

body 2

7 Alice dress

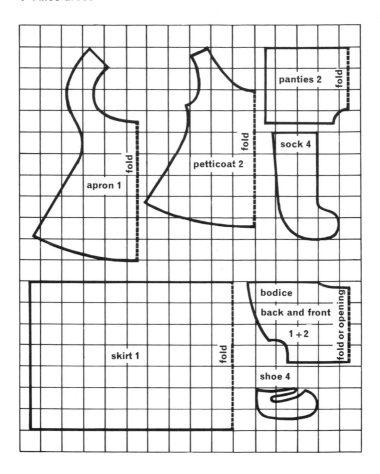

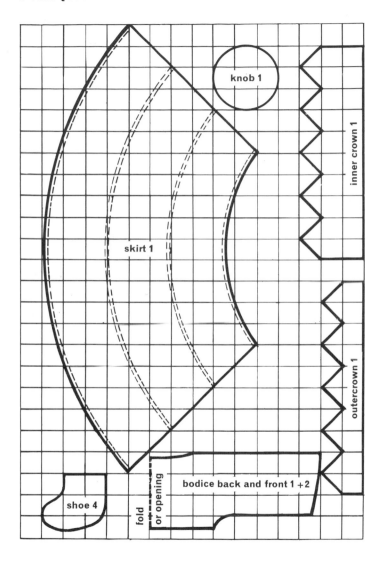

knob 1

inner crown 1

skirt 1

outercrown 1

shoe 4

fold

or opening

bodice back and front 1 +2

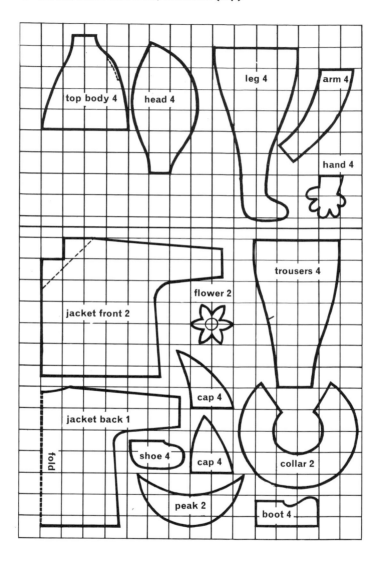

top body 4

head 4

leg 4

arm 4

hand 4

jacket front 2

flower 2

trousers 4

jacket back 1

fold

cap 4

shoe 4

cap 4

collar 2

peak 2

boot 4

10 Mermaid (tail)

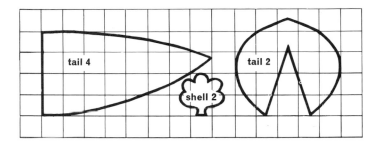

tail 4

shell 2

tail 2

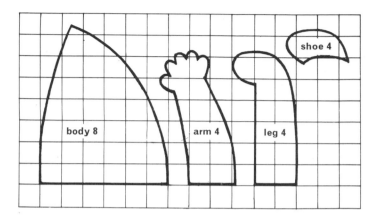

12 Cat

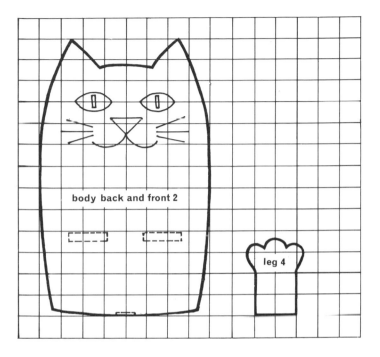

body back and front 2

leg 4

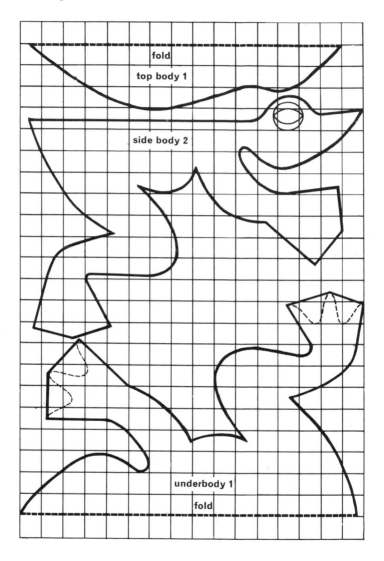

fold

top body 1

side body 2

underbody 1

fold

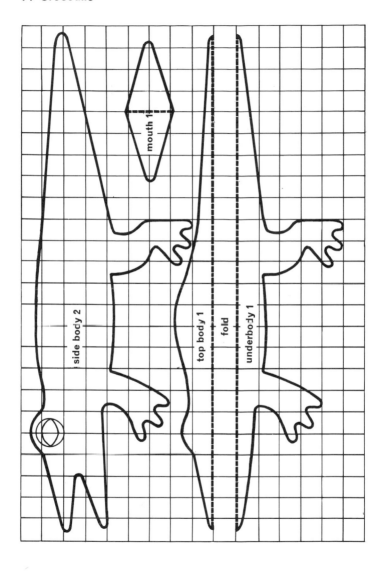

mouth 1

side body 2

top body 1

fold

underbody 1

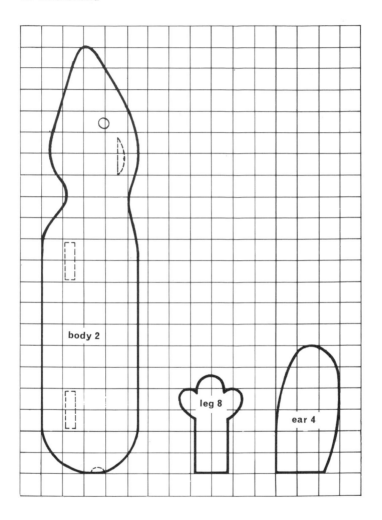

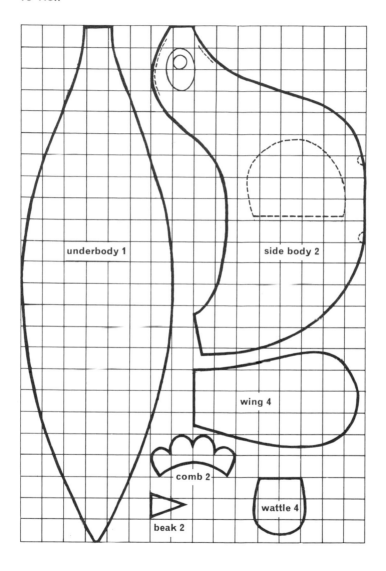

underbody 1

side body 2

wing 4

comb 2

beak 2

wattle 4

17 Chick

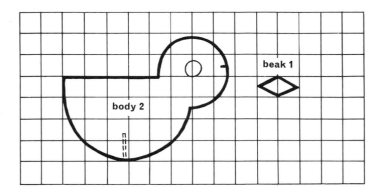

beak 1

body 2

18 Fish

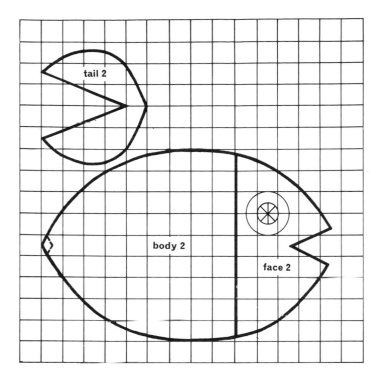

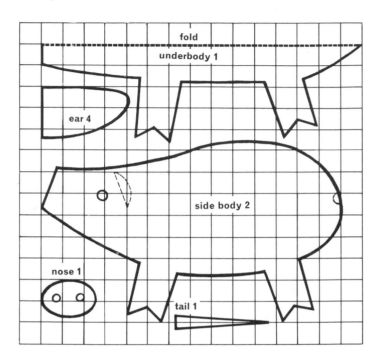

fold

underbody 1

ear 4

side body 2

nose 1

tail 1

20 Hobby horse

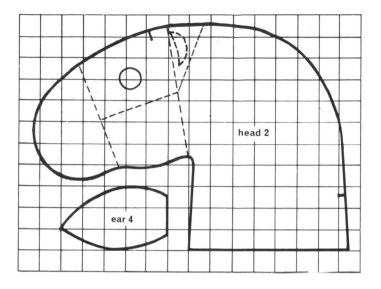

head 2

ear 4

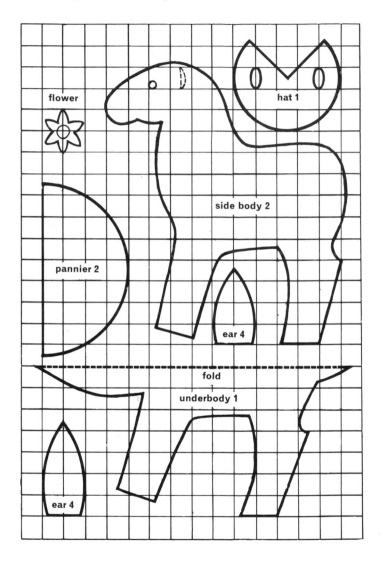

flower

hat 1

side body 2

pannier 2

ear 4

fold

underbody 1

ear 4

22 Hedgehog

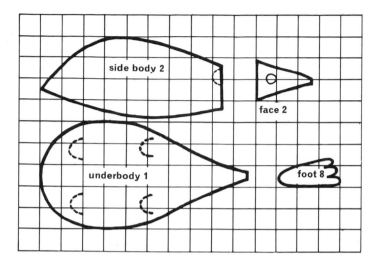

side body 2

face 2

underbody 1

foot 8